Ebb & Flow
A POETRY EXPERIENCE

Original poems by
TRICIA SYBERSMA

TRICIA SYBERSMA
Gratitude · Connection · Action

Dedicated to all those who choose to celebrate the magic of life

COPYRIGHT © 2022 BY TRICIA SYBERSMA
DESIGN AND LAYOUT BY RACHEL ROSSANO
ALL IMAGERY FROM SHUTTERSTOCK.COM

ALL RIGHTS RESERVED. NO PART OF THIS BOOK MAY BE REPRODUCED, STORED IN A RETRIEVAL SYSTEM, OR TRANSMITTED IN ANY FORM OR BY ANY MEANS—ELECTRONIC, MECHANICAL, PHOTOCOPY, RECORDING, OR OTHERWISE—WITHOUT THE PRIOR PERMISSION OF THE PUBLISHER OR AUTHOR.

THE ONLY EXCEPTION IS BY A REVIEWER, WHO MAY QUOTE SHORT EXCERPTS IN A REVIEW.

CONTACT THE AUTHOR AT: TRICIA@TRICIASYBERSMA.COM

PRINT ISBN: 978-1-948074-88-9

EBOOK ISBN 978-1-948074-52-0

FIRST EDITION

I invite you

...to experience poetry in a fresh, new way.

Put aside all thoughts and simply allow the ebb and flow of these stories to move you.

Invite them to ignite your imagination, creativity, and senses.

Allow them to take you somewhere.

Somewhere familiar; somewhere you've never been.

Let them show you how to welcome and ride the ebb and flow of your life.

After all, our stories are poetry in the ebb and flow of life itself.

Enjoy, *Tricia*

What's waiting inside

Bathed in the Moonlight

Treasures

Gather

Ebb & Flow

Here I sit

Divide

Within

Unknown

Hope

Bathed in the Moonlight

Full winter moon glistening on the Caribbean Sea

While gentle waves sing a lullaby for three

Bathed in the moonlight

Warm, salty breeze tickling bare skin

Laughing, playing, a night that will never end

Bathed in the moonlight

Silhouettes and shadows, softness, and beauty

Dancing and swaying, innocence awaking

Bathed in the moonlight

Touching, embracing

Reaching, searching

Sure, unsure

Is it magic or madness?

Bathed in the moonlight

Secrets, rituals
Sisterhood, motherhood
Nurturing, loving,
As we are

Bathed in the moonlight

*Chosen to be published with Polar Expressions

Treasures

What treasures will I find at the seaside today?

Some come looking for jewels and coins from a time long ago

Some come looking for answers to questions they will never know

Some come looking for magic and healing to miraculously unfold

What treasures will I find at the seaside today?

Will I find jewels and coins,

Magic and miracles hidden in the deep blue sea

Or will I find a treasure meant just for me?

The seaside welcomes me with a wide-open view

I start exploring to find what's new

I see purple flowers on bright-green vines

Winding their way through the pearly white sand

And a rainbow of colors in the sky so grand

I hear the birds chirping and squawking

The surf caresses my feet where I'm walking

I feel the breeze as it teases my dress as if longing

I smell the freshness of the wide-open sea

The seaweed as it dries in the sun

And the blossoms of the sea grape tree

I feel the warmth of the sun on my face and arms

The ocean spray like a kiss from a loved one

I taste the salt on my lips and breathe

And in my words as I describe what happened next

What treasures did I find at the seaside today?

Hidden in the seeing and feeling

The hearing, tasting and scent

I found the most precious treasure of all

I found me

At the seaside

Today

Gather

The first dawn we gathered
The first sunset we gathered

With the beat of the first drum, we gathered
Inside the first shelter we gathered

Harvesting and hunting we gathered
Preparing and sharing food we gathered

In storms we gathered
For safety we gathered

Welcoming a new life, we gathered
Saying goodbye to a loved life we gathered

In conflict we gathered
In unity we gathered

In sadness we gathered
In joy we gathered

In song and dance we gathered
Storytelling and celebration we gathered

Be it past or present
Be it near or far
When we gather

We gather friendships
We gather memories
We share, we laugh
We cry, we heal
We heal ourselves
We heal each other
We heal our communities
We heal the earth

To gather is connection
To gather is community
To gather is medicine
To gather is love in action

...Gather

*Chosen to be published with Polar Expressions
**Director's Award for Poetry 2021 with The Love Foundation

Ebb & Flow

The moon and tides

Where the sea melts into the sky

Day into night

Summer into fall

Winter into spring

Seasons to plant and harvest for all

Now and then

Rise and fall

Back and forth

Here and now

Micro and macro

Universe, multiverse

Home, on Earth

Oh my

To love and let go

To give and take

To start and finish

To hurt and heal

To harm and forgive

To laugh and cry

To live and die

To say hello and goodbye

The rise and fall of my breath

The loving beat of my heart

My tears and laughter

Happily ever after

It is rhythm and blues

The sway of slow dancing

It is rhyme and reason

The pause between seasons

It's the rolling seas

It's the wise willow tree

That know

The secret of life

Is to…

Ebb and flow

Here I sit

Here I sit watching you
knowing it's the last time

You will enjoy the hidden secrets in our back yard
You will sniff the musty scent of the earth
You will feel the gentle breeze on your fur
You will lay on the sun-warmed patio stones
You will drink the cool water from your bowl
You will nibble a tasty treat

Here I sit watching you
knowing it's the last time

You will feel the tickle of the grass under your paws
You will bark when the birds swoop down to play
You will listen to the water lapping against the side of the dock
You will sit quietly beside me as I write
You will feel my loving touch as I pat your sweet head
You will hear my soft words as you begin your new journey into the light

Here I sit watching you
with tears in my eyes

As you take your last breath
As you come to rest at peace
with this life

As I look up into the palm trees
and feel them guiding you
To take flight
Don't look back
Soar into the sky, into the light

Here I sit watching you
alone

I Know you are safe
I Know you are healed
I know you are free

I send you my love and gratitude
For all you taught me
Shared with me
And how you loved me

Here I sit watching you
believing

That you will be waiting to welcome me with your tail wagging
when we meet again

*Chosen to be published with Polar Expressions

Divide

Background sounds

Music people's voices

Water bubbling, laughing

Warm breeze tickling skin

Tired yet awake

Full yet hungry

Calm yet restless

What's next?

Clarity yet confusion

I'm alone yet not alone

A great divide, a great mystery

A great void, a great opportunity

Who, who, who will it be?

No one yet everyone

Written during lockdowns in 2021

Within

Why do we look up when we pray?

The beautiful, blue sky, sun, and the weather live up there
But all the great teachers tell us to look within

There is a universe in the sky up above
Solar systems, distant planets and mysteries live up there
But there is a mightier universe found within

The world can be a stormy place
Violence, turmoil, and confusion live up there
But one can always find peace waiting within

Why do we look up for answers?
Yes, information and opinions can be found up there
But true wisdom lives within

There are wonderful sights and sounds to enjoy up there
Mountains, forests, deserts, quiet streams and more
But the stillness of the soul lives within

How fortunate we are to have opportunities to enjoy and learn
And have amazing experiences up there
But our deepest personal adventures live within

When it's time to rest, to laugh, to heal and to be grateful
And you want to share it with your friends who live out there
Remember your best friend the one who always listens lives within

So where do I go when the world is too much? When I need to find
My teacher
My universe
My peace
My wisdom
My stillness
My destination
My personal adventures
My best friend
When I need to find myself

I look within

*Chosen to be published with Polar Expressions

The Unknown

I am taking a step
just a little step, a new step
Forward then backwards, to the left and to the right
In this new place, it is neither dark nor light

I ask myself, where am I? Please, someone?
And a quiet voice answers
In the unknown, my dearest one

I am taking a step, a bigger step now
Surrounded by new sights and new sounds all around
How will I know what's right and what's wrong?
The questions are mounting, where is the ground?

I ask myself, where am I?
And a calming voice answers
In the unknown, my curious one

I am taking a step and questioning now
What if I fumble? What if I fall?
What if I find answers and knowledge for all?

I ask myself, where am I?
And a strong voice answers
In the unknown, my bravest one

I am taking a step, one, now three
Exploring new lands, ideas, and me
There are no judgements, mistakes, or regrets
Instead, only learning and one giant quest

I ask myself, where am I?
And a loving voice answers
In the unknown, my evolving one

What wonders to see
And mountains to climb
Adventures to seek
For now, there is endless time

I ask myself, who am I?
And a spirit voice answers
You are my dearest one
curious and bravest one
evolving and growing
For the unknown is now your new calling

Chosen to be published with Polar Expressions

Hope

It's just after dawn and I'm sitting by the sea
The sun is rising to my left behind the old sea grape tree

Enjoying the morning shade as I sit on this step
With my feet in the cool sand as soon, the sun will heat up

I hear the little birds in the wise old tree
As they twitter and chirp good morning to me

The sea is gentle this early morning
With slow, sleepy waves that come rolling
To wake up the Earth because it's time to get up
As this brand-new day is about to start

Yes, it is a good time to write about hope

I am a girl, a woman, a daughter, a sister, a mother, and a friend
I have experienced changes, challenges, and tragedies all from within

Our stories unite us through our tears and our laughter
This is the human experience we are all after

We come into this life weak and vulnerable
Ready to fight, survive, yet remain loveable

Hidden in all our experiences is a promise
That keeps us true, trying, and honest

So, what is this promise that keeps us going?
A promise of deep yearning and knowing?
It is Hope!
How do I know this?
Because it is here all around me
Embracing me, strengthening me, healing, and teaching me
It never tires, never costs, never judges or discriminates

It is the sun rising every morning
It is the vast seas and the mighty mountains
It is the promise in each sprout and blossom

In challenges, sadness, and despair
In joy, thanksgiving, and celebration
I step outside to give thanks because
I know that Hope lives here

Chosen to be published with Polar Expressions

About the Author

TRICIA SYBERSMA

Tricia was born in Toronto and grew up in Blue Mountain, Ontario. In 1993, Tricia and her family moved to the Cayman Islands, where she continues to reside.

Whether surrounded by sandy beaches or snow, Tricia looks for the magic that is just beyond our awareness, then brings it to life with her poems and stories.

Tricia is a HeartMath® Certified Trainer

Visit TriciaSybersma.com

ABOUT THE DESIGNER – RACHEL ROSSANO

Rachel grew up in the beautiful Niagara Region in Ontario, Canada. She has been designing and art directing for 15 years and can be reached at RachelRossano.ca

Special thanks to Polar Expressions, who inspired me to play with poetry and helped me find a new form of expression.
www.polarexpressions.ca

www.ingramcontent.com/pod-product-compliance
Lightning Source LLC
Chambersburg PA
CBHW040758240426
43673CB00014B/384